Acclaim for *Unwrapping the First Christmas*

"I knew I needed to read this book after I failed the 10 multi—choice questionnaire on the Christmas story facts that is at the beginning of the book! I have been an Anglican minister here in New Zealand for 30 years. Anglicans really know how to do Christmas with the season of Advent, lots of 'nine lessons and carols' services, midnight Christmas services, etc. Somehow I had never thought about the facts that surround the season of Christmas and the traditions that have somehow attached themselves to the celebration of Jesus's birth. I think the wonder of this book is that it takes you back to what Christmas is really about – God becoming a man and living among us."
— Rev. Gradon Harvey, National Director for North-South, Anglican Minister, New Zealand

"Dr. Cooper has mixed real life and family—minded encouragement with thorough historical and scientific research in order to bring a rich and transformational

turn on the implications of the incarnation. For the faithful and the skeptic, for the scholar and the parent, here is miracle and reality as our Father surely intended."
— Dr. Neal F. Brower, Western District Superintendent, Evangelical Free Church of America

"This book is a must read for every Christian. Dr. Michael Cooper, unwraps beautifully the true meaning of celebrating Christmas. It gives the clear understanding of the festival called Christmas to the lay people and an in—depth study to the theologians. It uncovers the myths associated with Christmas and leads us to the true meaning of the first Christmas in Bethlehem."
— Pastor Vinod Abraham, Founder and President, SEWA, Punjab, India

"Dr. Cooper makes a convincing argument for the reliability of Christ's birth from a historical scientific perspective. I'm quite impressed."
— Pastor Matt Till, Restoration Church, Chicago, USA

"Seemingly every year many Christians wrestle with or casually accept the origins and traditions associated with Christmas. In this fine book Michael Cooper provides the reader with the relevant data and a concise discussion to sort through the issues. His analysis is both academically-informed and yet popularly accessible. Highly recommended."
— John W. Morehead, Adjunct professor, Multnomah University, Director, Multi-faith Matters

"Wow! This is a book we need to read if we want to dig deep into the historical and factual account of the first Christmas. I honestly thought I already had a good understanding of the Christmas narratives until I got to answer the questionnaires at the beginning of this book. The family devotional at the end is also very helpful. I would say this is a must-read book for every Christian. It's easy to read that when I started reading, I didn't stop until I finished."
— Bishop Chito Ramos, ABCCOP, Philippines

UNWRAPPING THE FIRST CHRISTMAS

Michael T. Cooper

EPHESIOLOGY PRESS

First published in 2019 by EPHESIOLOGY PRESS (http://ephesiology.com)

EPHESIOLOGY

MASTER CLASSES

eBook Edition, ASIN: B081Y535CB
Paperback Edition, ISBN: 9781712622698

Dedication

To the 37 percent of Christians who do not live in the Western world where Christmas lost its meaning. I pray your Christmas will be grounded in the history of the first Christmas.

And to the millions of others who are interested in the story of Christmas and America's fascination with Santa Claus.

As well as to the more than 60 percent of evangelicals who believe Jesus is the greatest being created by God.

Table of Contents

Acknowledgments

I've never written a book about Christmas although I have written about the historical events surrounding Jesus's birth. During my doctoral studies, I became acutely aware of certain Christian traditions with distinctly Pagan roots. Not that it was a concern, as I saw such similarities with what Paul attempted to do in Athens in connecting the philosophers to God (Acts 17). Nevertheless, it did cause me to think about the long—term impact of those traditions and new traditions evolving around Christmas on the vitality of the Christian faith in the Western world. Not that adherence to Christmas traditions is the cause of the decline of Christianity, because I believe many of those traditions are important in the life of the church.

So, I write this little book more as a testimony to how our family navigated Western Christmas traditions. Without our children, all adults now, I would not have given much thought to how traditions might impact faith. It is to their future families that I write. For our three, there will not be many new ideas since, as they would no doubt share with you, Daddy talks about these things every year. Nevertheless, I have them to thank for this book. Their inquisitive minds and challenging questions have always led to wonderful theological conversations.

It has been a privilege to work with four great men – Andrew, Matt, Devlin, and Arman. This book is also for them and their young families. I'll forever be grateful that they have allowed me to be a part of their lives. We collaborate on a project we call Ephesiology in our attempt to peel back the layers of Western culture that have piled on to our expression of church. You can learn more about this project at http://ephesiology.com and listen to our podcast by simply searching Ephesiology in your favorite podcast app. Be looking for the release of the book by William Carey Publishers on Leap Day 2020. Learn more about their books at https://missionbooks.org.

A special thanks to Michaela and Loré for their patience in meticulously reading the manuscript. The poor grammar and typos are still my fault, but I'm so grateful for their help.

Ultimately, this book is about a baby born more than 2020 years ago. He changed my world and . . . αὐτῷ ἡ δόξα καὶ νῦν καὶ εἰς ἡμέραν αἰῶνος (1 Pet 3:18b).

MTC

Preface

For years, Christmas has created a conflict between my academic self and my family self. Please don't get me wrong, our family absolutely loves Christmas. It actually might be our favorite holiday. We enjoy decorating the house – mostly inside as we try to keep Christmas simple. We'll put lighted electric candles in the windows, but that's about it for any outside decorations. Christmas carols are sung beginning in November for most of us, although Zachary believes they should be sung all year round. We select the perfect Christmas tree, usually in the most horrible weather possible. Loré unpacks our favorite ornaments and we carefully position them around the fir. The angel is gently placed at the pinnacle of the tree, nowadays by Christopher who towers above all of us. To complete our decorating, Michaela helps me lay the track for our O—gauge Lionel trains to circumnavigate the base of the tree.

The conflict for me is that I know 25 December is not when Jesus was born. I also know that first century

Christians did not celebrate His birth even though they knew about it because of Matthew and Luke's gospels. And, I know that some ancient Pagan celebrations and rituals have also found their way into Western Christian practices surrounding this auspicious occasion. Perhaps most disturbing of all, Christmas has become so commercialized that it is easy to forget the significance of God breaking into our world in what I have come to believe is the most incredible miracle ever so that His good news could be shared with all people, without discrimination.

I have had the wonderful privilege of traveling around a huge part of the globe. Inevitably I'll come across Christmas trees or Santa figures in churches or homes of Christians influenced by Western culture. I'll also see symbols of Western Christmas in local stores and street vendors where Hindu, Buddhist, even Communist Atheist shop keepers have no idea about the story of the first Christmas. Not too long ago, *60 Minutes* aired an episode about the enormous amount of Christmas decorations coming from China where people have no clue about the significance of the birth of a Savior who brought good news that is as much for the West as for them.

Christmas has become more of a cultural phenomenon highlighting the wealth of the West that is promised to all cultures as they celebrate this gift—giving, jolly old fellow, who miraculously spans the globe to distribute toys made by elves in his shop somewhere around the North Pole. I am absolutely convinced that this is not the story of Christmas that Jesus intended to be told, but it is the story that many cultures learn, and it becomes a symbol of Western Christianity, a Christianity that is foreign to Jesus. We are a Western world that has lost the meaning of the first Christmas.

This little book is not going to tell the whole Christmas story because in a real sense it is a story that we continue to experience today. My hope is that the book will help you with a deeper appreciation for the origin of Christmas and the spectacular miracle that happened in Bethlehem more than 2,020 years ago. It really is the most incredible miracle ever and the focal point of any genuine Christmas celebration. Who could have imagined that God Himself would appear in the flesh on that first Noël to tell us His story of love for people of every nation, tribe, and language? If only we could unwrap the first Christmas story from the layers of culture that shroud its beauty, we might actually experience the awe—inspiring story of how a baby changed everything.

There are only eight chapters plus a conclusion that are a mix between the academic with a bit of technicality, and the popular with anecdotes and reflections. I hope that it will be helpful to you as you navigate these issues with your family. Some of the content will be easier to share with children than others. The more challenging, academic content should help you with a firm foundation in the historical reliability of the story of that first Christmas.

My real hope, though, is that this book would make a difference for our brothers and sisters around the world. The Western expression of Christmas is largely a tradition as much attached to Western culture as to Western commercialization. We have Coca—Cola to thank for that. The traditions of the Christmas tree, many of our Christmas carols, even the myths surrounding Jesus's birth come from a particularly Western perspective and often do not reflect the story we discover in the Bible. I hope this little book will help you unwrap the first Christmas for yourselves.

Chapter One

How Well Do You Know the Christmas Story?

For years, right before Christmas break, I gave my students a simple 10 question multiple choice test to see how well they knew the story of Christmas. It wasn't intended to be a trick exam, but it certainly caused many a consternation as it became apparent that they didn't know the story like they thought.

So, how well do you know the Christmas story? Here are the 10 questions.

1) What did the angel Gabriel say to Joseph?
a. That Mary is pregnant by the Holy Spirit
b. That he will give the baby the name Jesus
c. a and b
d. Nothing

2) What mode of transportation did Mary and Joseph take to Bethlehem?
a. Donkey

b.   Wagon

c.   Train

d.   Don't know

3)   Who told Joseph that there was no room at the Inn?

a.   Inn Keeper

b.   Gabriel

c.   Mary

d.   No one

4)   Where in Bethlehem was Jesus born?

a.   In a manger located in a stable

b.   In the midst of animals and shepherds

c.   a and b

d.   In a manger, but we don't know where

5)   When did Mary give birth to Jesus?

a.   Immediately after they arrived in Bethlehem

b.   25 December

c.   On the way to Bethlehem

d.   After a few days upon their arrival in Bethle-hem

6)   How many wise men brought gifts and visited Jesus?

    a.   2

    b.   3

    c.   4

    d.   Don't know

7)   Where did the wise men visit Jesus?

    a.   At the manger after his birth

    b.   Together with the shepherds at the stable

    c.   At the Temple

    d.   In a house in Bethlehem

8)   How long did Joseph and Mary stay in Bethlehem?

    a.   Approximately two years

    b.   A few days because Joseph lost his job

    c.   Several months so that Mary could recover

    d.   40 days

9)   Where did Mary and Joseph go after Jesus' birth?

a.   Back to Nazareth

b.   To Egypt

c.   a and b

d.   To Jerusalem

10) Why did Jesus come to earth?

a.   To bring peace to the world

b.   To serve and give his life for many

c.   To save his people

d.   All of the above

How'd you do? Do you think you knew most of the answers? Perhaps all of them? My guess is that a few of you might have gotten all the questions correct, but most of you, I suspect, remember the Christmas story as portrayed in the sundry manger scenes we see in our neighbor's yards or from the Little Drummer Boy – my favorite Christmas program, by the way. Maybe you remember the story from the various carols we sing like "Away in the Manger" or "We Three Kings."

The myths surrounding our interpretation of the Christmas events are often colored by traditions and culture. So we are surprised when we learn that there really were not three wise men, or Mary did not travel by donkey, or there really wasn't an Inn in Bethlehem. But don't take my word for it, look at the story for yourself. Jesus's birth account can be found in Matthew 1:18—2:23 and Luke 1:5—2:40.

Oh yeah, I almost forgot. The answers to the questions are all "D." You can find my explanation for those answers in the appendix.

Chapter Two

The Myth of the Santa Story

It must have been two or three days before Christmas. As we always do, we collected the Christmas cards from friends and family into a basket and read them together as a family. On this instance, there must have been an inordinate number of cards with pictures of various Santas on them when suddenly Michaela saw a different one and exclaimed, "This one is from Jesus!"

We have wonderful memories of our kids and Christmas, as I'm sure you do as well. And as many parents do, we wrestled with what to tell our children about Santa. This was particularly challenging as our kids were very young while I was conducting my doctoral research. That research focused on the revitalization of an ancient religion called Druidry and as I became engrossed in its history and practices, I began to discover that my own faith traditions were being challenged. I'll get more into this in chapter four. That being said, we were uncomfortable in building up this culturally esteemed mythic figure we knew as Santa from our childhood because what would happen when our children discovered he wasn't a real person after all?

Children naturally fantasize. Their creative little minds can muster the most unusual circumstance or scenarios in their play. Some might reason that Santa is a part of this process. The mysterious person who appears at the end of a Thanksgiving Day parade can play an important role in a child's development, if for no other motive than to help children reason from fantasy to reality.

I have a foggy memory of when that happened for me. It was in the second grade as I held on to belief in Santa longer than most of my classmates. I actually recall being ridiculed around Christmas time that year as my little friends had far surpassed my level of intellectual maturity. It was one evening as I prepared for bed, maybe even Christmas Eve as I remember holding a cowboy boot with the expectation that Santa would fill it, when I decided to ask my mom about Santa. She kept the "party-line" – the Santa is real story – as long as she could, but I began to put things together that indicated he wasn't real after all: the reliable testimony of my elementary school friends; the fact that there were Christmas presents already under the tree; our tradition of opening a present on Christmas eve. All these began to point to the difficult reality that Santa didn't actually exist.

Well, for the most part, I turned out alright. I don't feel cheated in my childhood or irreparably scarred. The fact that I became an "insider" to the true story of the Santa myth didn't cause unnecessary inner turmoil, although I have heard cases where this occurred. But I wasn't from a particularly Christian family either. We didn't grow up going to church every Sunday, although we were certainly among parishioners on Christmas and Easter, as well as a few other special occasions that I can remember. So, Santa had very little impact on my faith. For our children, however, who grew up in a home where our identity came from our relationship with Jesus, the Santa myth could have had greater implications.

Think about it: Santa "knows when you are sleeping" gives us the impression that he is omnipresent; the fact that he has a list of names of good and bad children tells us he is omniscient; and the amazing speed by which he must travel to visit every Christian child in the world on Christmas Eve leaves us to believe he is omnipotent. Perceptive children might also conclude that Santa is eternal. After all, he was old when he visited their grandparents and he is still old when his jolly, round self amazingly comes down the fireplace, if you have one, with a huge bag of gifts. It isn't difficult to see how children might equate Santa with God or some other deity.

If we think about Santa in a different light, how can we explain the fact that millions of Christian children around the world will not receive any Christmas gift because their parents cannot afford one? If Santa gives gifts to good children, then all of those who do not receive gifts must be bad, so a little one might reason. The opposite might also be true. Just because a wealthy family can afford for Santa to give more gifts to their children doesn't necessarily mean that those children are good. Thus, Santa, for all the good he intends, can raise many questions.

When Santa's myth is exposed, it could be a short path to question God Himself who Scripture tells us is truly omnipresent, omniscient, and omnipotent, and offers the most amazing gift of eternal life – a gift far more valuable than one from Santa's North Pole toy factory. When he is outed by school friends, it can lead to mistrust between parents and children, as well as confusion about Christianity.

Now, it might be true that Santa can act as a bridge to God. Children will no doubt see images of Santa at the manger, bowing before the newborn King, with his bag of toys making him about 2020 years old. Parents can rightly use these opportunities to talk about the birth of Jesus. For our family, we decided to come clean and admitted early in our children's lives that Santa was a myth; just a cute story made up by well-meaning, although now very commercialized, adult intentions. Yet, the myth of the variously known Santa Claus – Père Noël, Father Christmas, Kriss Kringle, Weinachtsmann, Joulupukki – was based on a real person that lived nearly 1,700 years ago. So, we told them his story, the story of St. Nicholas.

Chapter Three

The Story of Saint Nicholas

You might think that there is as much myth surrounding St. Nicholas as the jolly old fellow we know today as Santa Claus. However, he actually was a real person. He was born sometime during the third century in the village of Patara on the southern coast of modern-day Turkey. The Apostles Paul and Barnabas first brought the gospel to the area around 47AD when they visited the cities of Lycaonia (Acts 14:6-7). In fact, Paul actually visits the city of Nicholas's birth in Acts 21:1 on his way to Jerusalem.

While there is some physical evidence – bones, icons, hagiography – that testify to Nicholas's life, there are many legends that emerged later in history. He becomes known as the patron saint of sailors and children. Due to family wealth, early traditions arose alluding to Nicholas's generosity. He is said to have thrown bags of gold into the windows of children and was responsible for raising three children from the dead as well as saving sailors from drowning. We'll discuss these in a moment.

His feast day corresponds to the most dangerous season to travel across the sea by ship, 6 December. Some suggest that Nicholas simply displaced Poseidon, the Greek god of the sea, as Christianity became the predominate religious expression in the fourth century and beyond.

His name raises many questions as well. Nicholas is derived from the Greek words *nike* and *laos* meaning "victory of the people." It was not a popular name for Christians largely due to its connection to the Nicolaitans the Apostle John writes about in Rev 2:6, 15. In the second century, Saint Irenaeus thought the Nicolaitans were a cult begun by Nicolaus, one of the seven chosen men in Acts 6:5. According to Irenaeus, the Nicolaitans exploited women as Nicolaus allegedly allowed extra-marital affairs with his own wife as a symbol of his complete abstinence from conjugal relations.

Such legends produce little assurance that Nicholas actually lived in the later third and early fourth centuries. As best we know, he never wrote a theological treatise or compiled a compendium of sermons.

Nevertheless, the long tradition of his presence at the council of Nicaea in 325AD suggests he indeed existed. In fact, recent scholarship clearly indicates Nicholas's presence at the first ecumenical council as evidenced by his name appearing on six lists of those in attendance. Most significantly, his name appears on Theodore the Lector's list (515AD) as Nicholas of Myra, the 115th named bishop in attendance (English 2018:311).

The oldest image of our legendary bishop dates from the mid 600s to 700s. Located today at St. Catherine's monastery in Egypt, the icon illustrates St. Nicholas along with Saints Paul, Peter, and John Chrysostom (English 2018:152). Chrysostom and Nicholas were contemporaries, although John was younger and likely more eloquent in speech as his name, Chrysostom (literally "golden mouth"), suggested.

Around the same time period as the icon, a monk and leader of a large monastery, Michael the Archimandrite, took on the task of writing a biography of St. Nicholas entitled *Life, Works, and Miracles of our Holy Father Nicholas, Archbishop of Myra in Lycia.* Drawing from two prior biographies no longer extant,

Michael describes the bishop as illuminating "the way ahead of us like a light-filled beam of the sun of justice, casting the radiance of his virtues like gold-gleaming rays" and stirring "lovers of the poor, and indeed those who love Christ and those who pardon humanity" (*Life* 1).

Nicholas became well-known for his charity. After his parents died, Nicholas inherited substantial wealth and used that for the good of the poor. Michael wrote, "Nicholas did not cease to continually hand over his abundance — to store it up in the secure treasure-houses of heaven" (*Life* 9). He wrote of a father who Nicholas helped rescue from poverty and from having to force his daughters into prostitution by providing three bags of gold thrown through a window on three different nights (*Life* 10-18).

Nicholas also defended the true doctrine of Christ against the heresies of Sabellius who did not believe in the Trinity, and Arius who believed Jesus was created (*Life* 25-26). He also led the charge against idols and Pagan temples, such as that of Artemis, that were so prominent in his city (*Life* 28-30). Nicholas could rightly be described as a bishop of justice as he stood in the gap to defend three men wrongly accused and sentenced to death (*Life* 31-32). We can rightly say that Nicholas represented the true marks of a Christian engaged in God's mission to make Him known through the defense of the faith, acts of justice, and proclamation of His glory to the nations (Rev 2:1-7).

There are always challenges when trying to wade through the stories of the saints. These hagiographies, as they are called, combine a grain of truth with incredible feats of healing or deliverance. Nicholas's story was not immune to this. Michael recounts,

When the fame of his holiness and care had been spread abroad to almost all the world and was being borne about on everyone's tongue because of these virtuous acts and good deeds and those like them, as is reasonable, some sailors, who were once sailing across the sea, when a mighty swell and storm suddenly arose against them by the plotting of a very fierce wind, saw that they were going to be altogether and completely subjected to a most inevitable danger of death. (Life 34)

No doubt his fame had spread as being a defender of the defenseless and a provider of the poor. He certainly rescued those in need, even in the time of famine:

> *When the saint received the grain and measured it, he distributed it to everyone as they praised God, who has power over all things, and it came about that the grain sufficed for those who received it from him for a period of two years, as a blessing. (Life 39)*

Nicholas was a remarkable person who loved Christ more than the world and gave everything for His sake. So, were these myths and legends created to inspire the faithful? Some, perhaps; others seem too fanciful to believe. Yet, juxtaposed to Santa, who travels 111 million miles in one evening at an estimated 3.6 million miles per hour on a sleigh with eight tiny flying reindeer – nine if you add Rudolph – then Nicholas's story seems far more plausible.

However, as we continue to unwrap the first Christmas, there is a story even more plausible; one that is well-documented and attested through time; one which is evidenced not only by eyewitness accounts but also by astronomical events that leave no room to doubt the birth of a Savior who is Christ the Lord

(Luke 2:11). Before we get to His story, let's take a moment to explore the Pagan origins of Western Christmas.

Chapter Four

The Pagan Origins of Western Christmas

Christianity faced many challenges in its early years. From threats by religious and political leaders to near riots by economic and social leaders, Christianity always seemed in dire straits. Yet the remarkable story of the early church was its resilience in the face of difficult circumstance. The growing band of Christ-followers were transformed by the Holy Spirit and empowered to tell the story of Jesus. The brilliance of those early years is revealed in the manner in which Christians were able to connect Christ with culture. Such a connection often resulted in social, religious, intellectual, economic, and political transformation (Cooper 2020).

Conditions dramatically changed when Christianity became the official religion of the Roman Empire in the fourth century. It is not unusual for a religion to take on the characteristics and customs of a culture over time. While Christianity became the dominant belief system of Europe from Classical Antiquity to the Middle Ages, it was not without having been profoundly influenced by its Pagan antagonists. In spite of efforts by the church to disassociate with native religious celebrations, the practices remained. Christianity had not successfully eradicated these influences which were so much a part of the people's lives. Ultimately, the church would concede to the practices and instill or infuse them with a Christian veneer. Folk rituals and festivals took on new Christian meaning as saints and martyrs replaced local deities (Jones 1998:85; Hillgarth 1987:325-327). The discontinuity between Christianity and ancient traditional beliefs did not exist as it had at the formation of Christianity in the first and second centuries.

The historian and biographer of Augustine, Peter Brown, noted that even in the church in the city of Hippo in North Africa, Augustine (354-430), one of the great theologians of the Western church, "felt that the quality of his own congregation had already been seriously diluted by the semi-pagans who had joined the church en masse, when Christianity became the established religion" (Brown 1967:234). By the end of the fourth century, the old religion of the Roman Empire was reviving. Symmachus, the Pagan prefect of Rome in 384, was calling for equality of religions just as had the Christians less than a hundred years before. While legal equality was fruitless to some degree in spite of successfully restoring the Altar of Victory in the senate house (Frend 1984:621), Symmachus's call indicated a continued traditional religionist voice in the city and a growing conflation of Christianity and Pagan traditions.

By the sixth and seventh centuries, missionaries were Christianizing folk religious expressions as well as sacred places under the papal direction of Gregory I (540-604) (Jones and Pennick 1995:75). The Venerable Bede (673-735), the father of English history, preserved the record of the great missionary pope in his *Ecclesiastical History of the English Nation*. Writing instructions to Mellitus, abbot to the Gauls, who was on his way to join Augustine of Canterbury in England, Pope Gregory stated,

> *That the temples of the idols in that nation ought not to be destroyed; but let the idols that are in them be destroyed; let holy water be made and sprinkled in the said temples, let altars be erected*

and relics placed. For if those temples are well built, it is requisite that they be converted from the worship of devils to the service of the true God; that the nation, seeing that their temples are not destroyed, may remove error from their hearts, and knowing and adoring the true God, may the more familiarly resort to the places to which they have been accustomed. (The Ecclesiastical History of the English Nation 1.30)

Nearly two hundred years after Augustine of Hippo's *City of God* (5th century AD), which was written in part as a response to the desire of Romans to return to pre-Christian worship, Pope Gregory I justified his actions by referring to practices of the Jews in the Hebrew Bible. He continued,

For there is no doubt that it is impossible to efface everything at once from their obdurate minds; because he who endeavors to ascend to the highest place, rises by degrees or steps, and not by leaps. Thus the Lord made Himself known to the people of Israel in Egypt; and yet He allowed them the use of the sacrifices which they were wont to offer to the Devil, in his own worship; so as to command them in his sacrifice to kill beasts, to the end that, changing their hearts, they might lay aside one part of the sacrifice, whilst they retained another; that whilst they offered the same beasts which they were wont to offer, they should offer them to God, and not to idols; and thus they would no longer be the same sacrifices. (The Ecclesiastical History of the English Nation 1.30)

The professor of medieval history, J. M. Wallace-Hadrill, commented that this letter indicated a change of papal missionary strategy in England. Gregory had become painfully aware of the ineffectiveness of the mission and accommodated to Pagan practices as much as possible (Hadrill 1988:44).

One hundred and fifty years after Gregory's missionary policy of accommodation, the missionary bishop Boniface from England – also known as the apostle of Germany – expressed his concern regarding the continuation of pre-Christian religious practices in Rome. Writing to Pope Zacharias (ca. 742), he stated,

Some of the ignorant common people, Alemanians, Bavarians, and Franks, hearing that many of the offenses prohibited by us are practiced in the city of Rome imagine that they are allowed by the priests there and reproach us for causing them to incur blame in their own lives. (Ep. 40)

A few years afterward, Pope Zacharias wrote to Boniface in response to questions regarding the rebaptism of people who had been baptized by priests continuing Pagan practices in their churches. Pope Zacharias alludes to Boniface's concern for such Pagan practices, writing "As to those sacrilegious priests who, you say, sacrificed bulls and goats to heathen gods, eating the offerings to the dead, defiling their own ministry . . . ." (Ep. 64). It seems apparent that Christianity struggled with the continuation of Pagan practices not only in Rome, but also all over the continent of Europe and in Great Britain. These Pagan beliefs and practices impacted the Christmas the West celebrates today.

To contemporary practitioners of Pagan religions like Druidry, three prominent Christian holidays, among many others, are in effect Christianized Pagan festivals: Christmas, Easter, and Halloween. The British historian, Ronald Hutton, pointed out that Christianity had no sacred calendar so one was developed based upon pre-Christian religions (1993:285). The new Christian celebrations provided a continuous reminder of the Pagan past and made it easy for people to adjust to the new religion. For example, the traditional date of 25 December for occidental Christmas coincides with the mid-winter festival of pre-Christian Pagan Europe. Between 17-24 December, Roman Saturnalia was celebrated in honor of Saturnus (Gr. Kronos), a Roman god of fertility. The cultural anthropologist Sir James Frazer (1854-1941) described events of Saturnalia surrounding the martyrdom of St. Dasius (d. ca. 303 AD):

> *Thirty days before the festival they chose by lot from amongst themselves a young and handsome man, who was then clothed in royal attire to resemble Saturn. Thus arrayed and attended by a multitude of soldiers he went about in public with full license to indulge his passions and to taste of every pleasure, however base and shameful. But if his reign was merry, it was short and ended tragically; for when the thirty days were up and the festival of Saturn had come, he cut his own throat on the altar of the god whom he personated. In the year A.D. 303 the lot fell upon the Christian soldier Dasius, but he refused to play the part of the heathen god and soil his last days by debauchery. The threats and arguments of his commanding officer Bassus failed to shake his constancy, and accordingly he was beheaded, as the Christian martyrologist records with minute accuracy, at Durostorum by the soldier John on Friday the twentieth day of November, being the twenty-fourth day of the moon, at the fourth hour. (1922:584)*

In 272 AD, Emperor Aurelian declared 25 December the birthday of the unconquered sun. *Sol Invictus*, as it was known, had long been observed in Syria and had gained popularity in the Roman Empire as people experienced pleasure from the religious rituals surrounding the festivities (Filotas 2005:32). When exactly the early church began celebrating the birth of Christ is unknown. While some, like Colin Chapman, an Islamic Studies scholar, suggested Pagans used 25 December in response to the Christian celebration, others, like Pagan Studies scholars Prudence Jones and Nigel Pennick, view the date as usurped from Pagans as a recognition of the "historical conflation of Christ, Mithras and Sol" (1995:76). Jones and Pennick are probably correct to assume that Christians expropriated the date. It is doubtful, however, that Christians conflated Christ with Mithras and Sol since the dating of these traditions and their similarities with Christianity suggest the opposite (Eddy and Boyd 2007). Similarly, as I have argued elsewhere (Cooper 2007) and will later argue in this book, Jesus was most likely born in the spring. Whether or not Christ was actually born in winter or spring, while important, does not detract from the issue of folk beliefs affecting Western Christian development, and especially Western Christmas traditions.

The mid-winter festival that eventually evolved into Christmas was celebrated in different ways all over Europe. Britain, Germany, and the Scandinavian countries celebrated the Yule feast recognizing the lengthening of the day and hoping for the beginning of a fertile year (Chapman 1990:31). While the Pagan name of this festival died out, the celebrations surrounding it remained intact. For example, decking the house with evergreens of various sorts was thought to provide protection from evil spirits (Jones and Pennick 1995:76). Food would also be left for particular spiritual beings like fairies or elves, a tradition preserved today in leaving cookies for Santa. The "Christmas tree" representing eternal life was decorated with candles to ensure the tree spirits would remain in the branches, and not affect the family.

Associated with ancient Druids, the mistletoe's magical qualities have long been recognized in the ancient world. An evergreen parasite that often kills its host tree, the mistletoe was a symbol of fertility and virility. The first century AD Roman historian, Pliny, recorded that the Druids revered the plant not only for its qualities, but also for its growth on oak trees. He wrote, "And indeed they think that anything which grows on an oak tree is sent from above and is a sign that the tree was selected by god himself." He goes on to describe the ritual associated with the plant,

> *In their language they call mistletoe a name meaning "all-healing." They hold sacrifices and sacred meals under oak trees, first leading forward two white bulls with horns bound for the first time. A priest dressed in white then climbs the tree and cuts the mistletoe with a golden sickle, with the plant dropping onto a white cloak. They then sacrifice the bulls while praying that the god will favorably grant his own gift to those to whom he has given it. They believe a drink made with mistletoe will restore fertility to barren livestock and act as a remedy to all poisons. (Natural History 16.249)*

English folklore dating from the seventeenth century attests to the use of mistletoe for decoration during the Christmas season. Along with other evergreen trees and bushes, mistletoe was believed to have power to protect homes. In some cases, homes might be haunted by goblins if the mistletoe were not removed by the end of winter (Hutton 1996:37).

The church of the Middle Ages struggled to maintain correct doctrine due to the influences and pressures it felt from the sundry traditions of very religious people. Throughout the history of the church, there has been a struggle between becoming syncretistic and maintaining orthodoxy. While the intentions of church leaders might have been pure, the end result was a weakened Christianity – even a confused Christianity – as Pagan religious traditions were incorporated into Christian practices and the distinction between the two became blurry.

So, what is the true story of Christmas, the story that this book is attempting to unwrap? Let's begin with the challenge of dating Jesus's birth.

Chapter Five

The Date of Jesus's Birth

Dating the first Christmas is nearly an impossible task for no clear date is given in the New Testament. Certain historical events recorded in Luke and Matthew's gospels, nevertheless, help in establishing a range for the possible date of the birth of Jesus Christ. If a range for the date can be established, then astronomical portents – such as the star of Bethlehem and the heavenly host – might help us be more precise. We'll address these in chapters six and seven.

For this chapter, we'll consider three important references to datable events in Luke's gospel. First, the birth of Jesus occurred during the reign of Caesar Augustus. His reign can be clearly dated between 15 March 44 BC to 19 August 14 AD (Luke 2:1). However, these dates are much too broad to be of help, but at least give us our first historical point of reference.

Second, Luke agrees with Matthew that the events took place "in the days of Herod the king" (Luke 1:5). Like Caesar's, the end of Herod's reign can be pinpointed fairly accurately to 4 BC. The Jewish historian Flavius Josephus relates that the very night of Herod's death there appeared an eclipse of the Moon, the only eclipse recorded by Josephus (*Antiquities* 17.6.4). This eclipse of the Moon was in the constellation Virgo and can be dated at 12-13 March 4 BC.

Third, Luke stated that the birth occurred during the time of a census (Luke 2:1). It was such a census that demanded Joseph's trip to Bethlehem from Nazareth along with Mary who was pregnant with Christ. Both were of the household of David and both needed to return to the city of David as the census required. The text specifically refers to a census around the time of Quirinius's governorship of Syria. Still, dating such a census has become problematic for pinpointing the birth event.

There are two possible dates for the time of Quirinius's governorship: 6-7 AD and 4-1 BC. However, the text can be literally translated as, "before [*prote egeneto*] the governorship of Quirinius" (Luke 2:2). If this is the proper translation, there still must be evidence to corroborate it. A number of such instances from Egypt indicate that Roman censuses took place every fourteen years. Knowing that Quirinius was governor in 6-7 AD and a census most certainly took place at that time, a prior census must have occurred in 8-7 BC. Leon Morris noted, "Certain inscriptions show that between 10 and 7 BC Quirinius performed military functions in the Roman province of Syria" (1997: 91). As such, Luke's account can be understood as a census before Quirinius' governorship, but during his military duties in Syria between 8-7 BC. All of these factors – Herod's death, Quirinius's governorship, Roman census – point to a birth sometime around 7 BC but no later than 4 BC.

Luke's account again helps in narrowing the time period by stating, "And in the same region there were shepherds out in the field, keeping watch over their flock by night" (2:8). Rabbinic law suggested that such flocks could be used for temple sacrifice and perhaps might indicate a birth near the time of a Passover. It was also common for flocks to be kept outside between April and November when the weather permitted. However, as Marshall pointed out, it should not rule out a mid-winter date for nothing in the text explicitly indicates a time of year (1978:108).

The early church did, however, suggest dates. For instance, a third century testimony by Hippolytus gave a mid-winter date of 25 December, and in the fourth century St. Chrysostom confirmed the date. Nevertheless, there are interesting issues with such a date as I noted in the previous chapter since it corresponded to *Sol Invictus*, established by Emperor Aurelian in the early third century, as well as to the Iranian inspired Roman mystery religion of Mithras. This should not strike us as strange as early Christian practices attempted to appropriate important Pagan holidays in order to bridge religious cultures. One second century Christian writer, though, suggested a spring date. Clement of Alexandria (ca. 170 AD) stated, "And there are those who have determined not only the year of our Lord's birth, but also the day; and they say that it took place in the twenty-eighth year of Augustus, and in the twenty-fifth day of Pachon" (*Stromata* 1.21). This date corresponds with 20, 21 April in the Gregorian calendar.

As mentioned, the New Testament historical evidence suggests the narrowing of the possible range of dates for the birth of Christ to the spring of 7-4 BC. Yet, there were possibly two additional events that occurred in the sky that might help determine the date of Jesus's birth: the heavenly host in the Gospel of Luke chapter 2 and the star in the Gospel of Matthew chapter 2. With such a timeframe in mind and additional details, we can begin to search for particular astronomical events that would be suggestive for the birth of Christ, the subject of the next two chapters. Such astronomical events should not surprise us. As Alexander Toepel has noted, Jews were well acquainted with Greek astrology during the Second Temple period (2005: 231). So, it is not unusual to find references to the stars. First, let's look at the Nativity according to Luke.

Chapter Six

The Nativity in Luke

Years ago, Dr. Michael York, now retired professor from the Centre for the Study of Cultural Astronomy and Astrology located at Bath Spa University in England, invited me to write an article about the relationship between Christianity and astrology. The request interested me on multiple levels. For one, Dr. York was not a Christian. He was a practicing Pagan. For another, the article would be published in an edition of an academic journal focusing on the scientific study of astrology. So, I accepted the invitation and began to research Christianity's relationship to astrology. In that pursuit, I naturally came to two important events surrounding the birth and infancy of Jesus: the appearance of the heavenly host to the shepherds and the visit of the wise men from the East who had followed a star to Bethlehem.

The following two chapters explain more about these important events and their meaning. First, in distinction from today, it is important to note that ancient astrology was considered a respectable science. So, I am not advocating the practice of astrology, but simply understanding how the first century hearers of the gospel accounts would have understood the astrological significance.

Luke's account of Jesus's birth is the most complete account in Scripture. From the angelic visitation with Mary to the miraculous birth of Jesus, Luke provides details that are nothing short of amazing. We pick up his story with the angelic announcement of the birth of Christ to shepherds tending their flocks. He writes, "And suddenly there was with the angel a multitude of the heavenly host praising God and saying, 'Glory to God in the highest and on earth peace among those with whom he is pleased'" (Luke 2:13-14).

Luke's heavenly host is often thought to refer to other angels that joined with the angel who announced the birth to the shepherds. "Heavenly host" is a Lukan *dis legomenon*, simply meaning that only Luke uses the phrase in the New Testament, and it is only used twice. In Luke 2:13 the phrase is rendered *stratias ouraniou*, literally an army from or of heaven. The phrase is used a second time in Acts 7:42. The Acts of the Apostles makes up the second volume of Luke's historical account of the ministry and deity of Christ and his disciples. In chapter seven, he relates the testimony of Stephen, a Jewish Christian, before he is stoned to death by Jewish religious leaders. Luke records, "But God turned away and gave them over to worship the host of heaven" (Acts 7:42).

The host of heaven, *te stratia tou ouraniou*, has an obvious interpretation of the stars and planets to a first century Greek reader. This understanding corresponds with the Gentile focus of both Luke and Acts; Luke is writing to a Roman official, the most excellent Theophilus (Luke 1:3), who certainly understood astrological language in the texts. The understanding also corresponds with what other biblical literature offers as the meaning of the phrase (2 Chron 33:3, 5; Neh 9:6; Jer 8:2; 19:13; Zeph 1:5). For example, 2 Chronicles records that Manasseh worshipped the host of heaven and built two altars for the practice in the Temple. The Chronicler wrote,

> *For he rebuilt the high places that his father Hezekiah had broken down, and he erected altars to the Baals, and made Asheroth, and worshiped all the host of heaven and served them . . . . And he built*

> *altars for all the host of heaven in two courts of the house of the Lord. (2 Chron 33:3, 5)*

Ignatius of Antioch (AD 30-107), a contemporary of Luke who no doubt knew the Apostle Paul, writes in his so-called Star Hymn a testimony to this early understanding,

> *A star shone forth in heaven above all the other stars, the light of which was inexpressible, while its novelty struck men with astonishment. And all the rest of the stars, with the sun and moon, formed a chorus to this star, and its light was exceedingly great above them all. (Letter to the Ephesians, XIX)*

Ignatius' account is significant. Writing to Christians in the city of Ephesus, Ignatius made an early reference to both Matthew and Luke's nativity accounts. What is more, Ignatius was the bishop of the church at Antioch, the city where both Matthew and Luke's gospels were believed to have been written. There is also a tradition that places Antioch as the home city of Luke, although Troas in Asia Minor is more likely (Cooper 2020). It then is reasonable to assert that Ignatius had first-hand knowledge of both Saints Luke and Matthew, perhaps even knew them personally, which adds additional credibility to their gospels' Nativity accounts as well as to Ignatius himself. Thus, Ignatius is reading the gospels from the perspective of someone who understood both the language usage and the culture. It seems reasonable to suggest that the first and second century readers or hearers of the astronomical signs in the gospels would have understood them as the stars and planets.

The objection might be made that the heavenly host were in fact angels. After all, "Angels We Have Heard on High" is one of the standard Christmas carols. Luke 2:15 says, "When the angels [*oi angeloi*] went away from them into heaven, the shepherds said to one another, 'Let us go over to Bethlehem and see this thing that has happened, which the Lord has made known to us.'" The phrase, "the angels," can be understood in two ways. First, *oi angeloi* is the plural of *angelos* which can be rendered as messenger. For example, Luke 7:24 states, "When John's messengers [*ton angelon*] had gone, Jesus began to speak to the crowds concerning John: 'What did you go out into the wilderness to see? A reed shaken by the wind?'" Messengers is the plural genitive of *angeloi*. Not only in Luke 7, but we also see *angelos* translated as "messenger" in Luke 9:52.

Second, *oi angeloi* could literally be angels. Saint Augustine in *Harmony of the Gospels* (II.V.XVII) and St. Basil in *On the Spirit* (XVI) understand the account as such. This second understanding fits appropriately with Luke's heavenly host due primarily to a first century cultural understanding. If the interpretive word for the passage is "angel" rather than "messenger," it is important to understand that ancient literature connects angelic beings with the planets (Toepel, 2005: 231-238). Commenting on a Qumran fragment (4Q405) of the *Songs of the Sabbath Sacrifice*, Von Struckrad states, "In line 12 of this fragment the angels' 'turning of their paths' are mentioned, 'when they rise, they rise in a wonderful way.' This probably refers to the planets' turning points that were of prominent importance for Babylonian astronomical calculations" (2000:12). This understanding, then, would be consistent with the observations and understanding of Luke's shepherds.

If the heavenly host is indeed a reference to the planets or other heavenly bodies, then we might consider looking for astronomical events that occurred at that specific time that will help us pinpoint Jesus's birth. Michael Molnar, a former astronomer from the Physics and Astronomy Department at Rutgers University, suggests that a significant astronomical event would have been an occultation – an incident when one planet passes behind another – of the planet Jupiter by the Moon in the constellation of Aries. According to ancient astronomer Claudius Ptolemy (100-170AD), Aries had long been associated with Judea. These particular astral portents would seem to fit with Luke's account of the heavenly host, but they do not seem as spectacular as the text suggests. Nevertheless, two such occultations occurred in our 7-4BC timeframe for the nativity; first on 20 March and then again on 17 April 6 or 5 BC. According to Molnar, of the two occultations, the 17 April 6 BC occultation while the Sun was exalted in Aries along with Jupiter pointed to the birth of a king in Judea.

In and of itself, this sign would not necessarily be significant. However, Molnar notes that not only were Jupiter and the Sun in Aries, but also Saturn and the Moon. It is worth noting that Venus was in Pisces and

Mars and Mercury were in Taurus. The seven celestial bodies that are observable with the naked eye where all amassed in the sky on the same date. According to Molnar, such a massing of the planets,

> *Blatantly point to a regal birth. Moreover, given that these extraordinary astrological conditions happened when people were hoping for freedom from tyranny and salvation from pagan intrusions, it is evident that the sky on April 17, 6 BC would have been thought to signal not just the birth of a Judean king but the anticipated birth of the Messiah. (1999:101)*

Molnar argues that such an astral portent occurring at this time had more regal significance than the births of the Roman Emperor Hadrian or even Caesar Augustus (1999:99). However, such a massing would have been spectacular to the shepherds only if it were in a darkened sky. Luke states that the shepherds were in their fields sometime between sunset and sunrise (*noctos*). Molnar asserts that before sunrise on 17 April the astronomical conditions of the sky were equally suggestive of a regal birth. He supports the significance by quoting from Vettius Valens' (120-175AD) description of royal births, "When the Moon [is present in the Ascendant and] if the star of Kronos [Saturn] should also be present, he [the native] will lead many countries. If the star of Zeus [Jupiter] should also be present . . ., they will become great kings" (in Molnar 1999:100).

It might make us uncomfortable to think that the Bible contains references to astrology, but don't think of astrology as what it later became. In Luke's time, astrology was very much looked upon as a science of sorts. It was not unusual, even as Christianity spread, that Christians would look to astrology as God ordained portents, or signs, of things to come. For example, the Irish missionary monk Colmcille (521-597AD) used astrology to determine the best time for his son to begin his studies (Ellis 1994: 243). For Raymond of Marseilles (12th century astronomer), astrology was to be understood in the context of God's sovereignty. Nothing in the heavens took place without the knowledge of God (Clark 2001: 93-94).

According to Ronald Hutton, by 1320AD, Western intellectuals considered the planets as deities controlled by God believing that Christians could legitimately use the planets to gain understanding for their future (Hutton 2003). A friend and colleague of 16th century reformer Martin Luther, Philip Melanchthon's interests in astrology was in relationship to medicine while rejecting astrology's fatalism. Johannes Kepler, well known for his theories of planetary motion, would attempt to harmonize astrology and theology (Montgomery 1963: 256-257).

The significance of the events surrounding the first Christmas cannot be underestimated. In God's relentless pursuit of a relationship with people, He did the unexpected and told a group of unsuspecting bystanders, the shepherds, about the birth of the Savior and the world changed in a flash. That message is still being announced today. My prayer is that we will be faithful in telling it, stripped of any cultural particularity, and unafraid of modern presuppositions related to astrology, so that people around the world will know that Christmas is a story of a Savior who is for all people and not about the mythic figure named Santa. The massing of the heavenly host of planets was a spectacular natural (general) revelation from God, and clearly indicated the birth of a great King who brought good news for all people.

The heavens declare the glory of God, and the sky above proclaims His handiwork. Day to day pours out speech, and night to night reveals knowledge. There is no speech, nor are there words, whose voice is not heard. Their voice goes out through all the earth, and their words to the end of the world. (Pslam 19:1-4)

Now, can you hear the heavenly host singing?

"Glory to God in the highest,

and on earth peace among those with whom he is please!" (Luke 2:14).

Chapter Seven

The Star of Bethlehem in Matthew

As I mentioned earlier, my favorite Christmas program is *The Little Drummer Boy*. Based on a 1941 carol written by Katherine Davis, it came to television in 1968. That is when I first saw the stop-motion animation that became popularized with *Rudolph the Red-Nosed Reindeer* four years prior. As the story goes, Aaron, a young Jewish boy orphaned when bandits killed his parents and stole their livestock, joins Ben Haramed's traveling caravan as Aaron's drum playing made the animals dance. If you haven't seen the show, I don't want to spoil it for you, but, to make a long story short, ultimately Aaron's pet lamb, Baba, is critically injured when run over by a Roman chariot. In hopes that the Magi could help the lamb, Aaron goes to them only to discover that there is a newborn baby who might heal Baba. Aaron, having nothing of material value to offer baby Jesus, plays his drum. He gave what he had in worship of the swaddled babe lying in a manger.

While it is absolutely an embellishment on the story of the Nativity, the point cannot escape us: these wise men, along with Aaron, gave all that they had. As much as I would like to believe, there is no doubt that there wasn't a little drummer boy who played his "drum for him, pa rum pum pum pum" However, there were actual Magi who left their homeland in search of the baby who is the King of kings.

Only Matthew's gospel records the visit of the Magi (*magoi*). Their identity remains a mystery, but it is certain that the wise men, who came from the East, had a keen sense of the stars. Some have suggested that they were Zoroastrian priests while others have maintained they were Chaldeans. The Greek word *magos* itself is only used six times in the New Testament, four of which are in Matthew's infancy account of Jesus. The other two occasions, found in Luke's second volume (Acts of the Apostles), are in reference to a Jewish "false prophet" who was most likely a part of the court of the proconsul Sergius Paulus. Elymas, the "wise man" (*magos*) opposed Paul and Barnabas as they were discussing the word of God with the proconsul. Sergius Paulus was obviously engaged in the subject matter, and Paul, annoyed with Elymas's attempt to turn the proconsul away from faith, declared, "And now, behold, the hand of the Lord is upon you, and you will be blind and unable to see the sun for a time" (Acts 13:11). More than likely, Elymas was a Jewish astrologer serving in the court of the proconsul. The loss of his sight would render him incapable of predictions based on astronomical observations.

Regardless of who the Magi are, it is clear that they knew astronomy and utilized their knowledge in an astrological manner. Matthew recorded the events as such:

Now after Jesus was born in Bethlehem of Judea in the days of Herod the king, behold, wise men from the east came to Jerusalem, saying, "Where is he who has been born king of the Jews? For we saw his star when it rose and have come to worship him." When Herod the king heard this, he was troubled, and all Jerusalem with him; and assembling all the chief priests and scribes of the people, he inquired of them where the Christ was to be born. (Matt 2:1-4)

After listening to the king, they went on their way. And behold, the star that they had seen when it rose went before them until it came to rest over the place where the child was. When they saw the star they rejoiced exceedingly with great joy. (Matt 2:9-10)

If we think chronologically, Luke's account of the Nativity precedes Matthew's account as Matthew appears to indicate that Jesus could be around two years old when the Magi come to visit (Matt 2:16). There are of course three possibilities for the Magi story: it could be myth, a miracle, or an astronomical event.

As for a myth, Richard Trexler has noted that the feast of kings (or Magi), traditionally observed on 6 January, could have pre-Christian roots. It was not unusual, as we have seen, for the early church to usurp significant Pagan holidays as their own. For example, Trexler suggests that themes found in Egyptian rituals, such as the commemoration of the virgin birth of Aion or the blessing of the Nile with its water turning to wine, parallel those found in Christianity (1997:9). Nevertheless, one must distinguish between ritual practices and beliefs that emerge after an event from the actual event. That is, many of the stories that some claim are similar to the story of Jesus and His birth – a god becoming flesh, alleged virgin births – cannot be dated with any accuracy to a time before the first Christmas. In other words, these accounts are most likely usurped from Christianity rather than the other way around.

As for a miracle, that is certainly a plausible explanation, but also one that cannot be proven without some form of evidence. In this case, we might have the eyewitness accounts of the Magi along with their traveling caravan – excluding Aaron and Ben Haramed of course. The Bible certainly provides a witness to the event, although not an eyewitness account; Matthew's information is at least second-hand. Undoubtedly, if it were a miracle there would be little hesitation in retelling the story of the star and it would have spread to willing listeners. Yet, what if the event actually happened? If astronomical evidence might help illuminate the biblical story of the birth of a king, then some standard for explaining the phenomenon would be important. An astronomer from the European Space Astronomy Centre in Madrid, Spain, Mark Kidger (1999:248), outlines the following criteria:

1. The explanation must be compatible with the probable date of the Nativity (we have determined this to be between 7-4 BC).

2. It must be a singular, special, or spectacular event.

3. It must be a rare event.

4. It must have had a special meaning for the Magi.

5. It must have occurred in the east.

6. It must have endured for some time.

In Greek, star (*aster*) has three possible translations: star, planet, or morning star. Many suggestions for the star have been offered ranging from the comet Haley to an eclipse of the moon. Whatever the star was, it was significant enough for the Magi to travel from the east to Jerusalem. Molnar (1999) suggested that the star was an aspect of a massing of planets in the constellation Aries as we saw as a feasible explanation for the heavenly host in Luke's account. While a massing of planets is astronomically spectacular and astrologically meaningful, it does not seem to fit with Matthew's account. Matthew is clear, the Magi saw a "star," not a massing of "stars." This would not necessarily mean that they did not know of a massing of planets in Aries. Certainly as trained astrologers they did, and certainly they understood a massing of planets as a portent to the birth of the King in Judah. Nevertheless, it was a star that compelled them to travel to Palestine.

Based on ancient descriptions of astronomical events, Kidger suggested that the star was a nova recorded by the Chinese and Koreans, but most certainly observed by the Magi. The Chinese astronomical documentation records a bright object, visible for nearly three months, as having appeared in the east in mid-March 5 BC. Interestingly enough, it was the Soviet-era scientist, B.V. Kukarin, who initially suggested that the Chinese record was that of the star of Bethlehem. However, his conclusion was that the Chinese had observed Venus. Venus, the planet associated with the mother of the gods in the Babylonian pantheon, would have been too common of an occurrence to have been the star. The bright object the Chinese observed, now known to have been a nova, fits the criterion of being a single astronomical event as Matthew's account records.

The time it would take for the Magi to travel from Babylon to Jerusalem was nearly two months (ca. 550 miles). This indicates that the star had to have been in the sky for at least this amount of time, if not more. If such is the case, a short-lived phenomenon, such as a comet or meteor shower, must be ruled out. Thus, the Chinese observation of the nova would best fit the scenario painted by Matthew. Kidger commented,

> *The most interesting aspect of this scenario is that the Star, which was in the east when first seen, would no longer be in the east upon their arrival. Every two weeks the Star would have risen an hour earlier until, two months later, it would have been almost exactly in the south at dawn. When the Magi set out for Bethlehem, they would have seen the Star before them in the south at dawn. (1999: 262)*

The detail given in Matthew's account sufficiently demonstrates that the observation of the Magi was an astronomical event consistent with the movement of the heavens. The Magi stated that they had seen the star rising in the east. As David Hughes (1976) noted, this would refer to a heliacal rising of the star. That is, the star was near to the sun (as cited in Kidger 1999:

26). Its movement across the sky from east to ultimately southwest is also consistent with being an astronomical event. Molnar offers a possible translation of Matt 2:9-10 from an astrological point of view. Adjusting for the event being a nova, the text could read: "And behold the planet [star] which they had seen at its heliacal rising went retrograde and became stationary above in the sky (which showed) where the child was" (1999: 96).

According to Kidger, the Magi would have actually seen a series of astronomical events which were significant. This series occurred over the course of three years leading up to the birth of Christ. First, a triple conjunction – a phenomenon where a planet or planets are observed in proximity to each other in a short period of time – of Jupiter and Saturn in 7 BC would not have been especially spectacular but would have attracted the attention of the Magi. The first such conjunction occurred in May in the constellation of Pisces. Kidger notes, "Knowing that Pisces was the constellation associated with the Jews, they would have followed this development with some interest, though probably they were not overly excited because they had seen something similar many times before" (1999:254). Molnar points out, however, that the notion of Pisces being the constellation of the Jews is a later development. In fact, Claudius Ptolemy (100-170AD), offers the understanding of the 12 constellations' associations with various countries or regions. He writes what may be from a second century BC source and clearly connects the constellation Aries with Judaea,

> *Let this be our brief exposition of the familiarities of the planets and the signs of the zodiac with the various nations, and of the general characteristics of the latter. We shall also set forth, for ready use, a list of the several nations which are in familiarity, merely noted against each of the signs, in accordance with what has just been said about them, thus:—*

> *Aries: Britain, Gaul, Germania, Bastarnia; in the centre, Coelê Syria, Palestine, Idumaea, Judaea. (Tetrabiblios 2.3)*

If an interpretation of the astronomical events is offered, it must be from the perspective of those who were there or who wrote about what was being interpreted. That is to say, Ptolemy's sources does not permit Judaea's connection with Pisces. Although, in Jewish astrology, the 12 constellations were often connected to the 12 tribes. Nevertheless, Molnar rejected the notion of a conjunction in Pisces yet admits that "the dashed outline of the sign Aries extends into the constellation Pisces and maybe Taurus" (1999:93). That is to say, due to the proximity of Aries to Pisces, one might be confused as to where the actual astronomical events were observed. So, if there were confusion, Kidger's hypothesis related to Pisces becomes interesting, an hypothesis noted by Johannes Kepler in the seventeenth century (Rosenberg 1972).

A second conjunction in September of 7 BC, might also have been observed by the Magi in the constellation Pisces. Finally, less than a month later, the planets, after a brief separation, began to approach each other for a third time on 4 December 7 BC. Up to this point in a 900-year time period, there had been seven triple conjunctions, only three of which occurred in Pisces. Considering that the Magi might not have been aware of a Jewish prophecy predicting the Messiah, only the triple conjunction in 7 BC would have been a significant portent of His arrival. This appears to be consistent with Luke's account of the heavenly host.

The Magi, presumably, would have reasoned that something significant was about to occur in Palestine. Jupiter, the royal planet, would have signaled the birth of a king. Saturn, the malign planet, marked perhaps the immanent death of a king. Kidger speculates that this in and of itself was not enough to set the Magi on their journey. They would have waited for a second sign, one that came not too long after the first. In February 6 BC a massing of planets occurred in Pisces. This time, along with the royal planet Jupiter, came Saturn and the planet of war, Mars. A year later a third sign would occur. In February 5 BC Jupiter paired with the two-day-old Moon in Pisces. Not far from them was another pairing in Pisces: Saturn and Mars. This would have convinced the Magi that something was about to happen in Palestine. Kidger observes,

> *One possible interpretation of the events would be the following. Jupiter is a royal and benevolent planet, while Saturn is malign and Mars invokes thoughts of war. The encounter between Jupiter and Saturn could have suggested to the Magi that a great ruler (the awaited Messiah) would arise,*

challenging a malign one (the Roman Empire), and liberate his country by the sword (as signified by bloody color of Mars). This interpretation would have been in tune with what they would have expected from the oracle of Balaam. (1999: 257)

Not long after the two pairings, an occultation occurred with Jupiter and the Moon in Pisces, an astronomical portent that could have been witnessed by the Magi. This occultation would have been particularly significant because it would have foretold the birth of a king in Judea.

So, the massing of several heavenly bodies and the nova of 5 BC all pointed to a spectacular, even miraculous, occurrence accurately documented, not only in the sky, but in both Luke and Matthew's accounts of Jesus's birth. It is a ton of information to digest, but it is extremely important for the historicity of Jesus Himself as well as the reliability of the biblical accounts of the heavenly host, the visit of the Magi, and the star they followed. Establishing such accuracy in the biblical documents gives us assurance that the events were not mythic creations such as what we see with Santa. These historical and biblical events actually happened, and they point to an extraordinary person – Jesus Christ – who came into our world just as real as any historic figure. He alone is the true meaning of Christmas and its central, even singular, focus. And, just like the Magi and the story of the Little Drummer Boy, Jesus is the one that draws our family's devotion. We hope He draws yours too.

Chapter Eight

A Christmas Devotional for Your Family

Advent simply means "arrival." During the Christmas season, many Christians in the West and around the world prepare for Jesus's advent during a period of four to five weeks leading up to the traditional date of Christmas morning. Ever since our kids were small, we celebrated with an Advent wreath at the dinner table with four candles surrounding it and one in the middle. Each week we would read a passage of Scripture, light a candle, pray, and sing a Christmas carol. We weren't super legalistic about it or even regular, but we did instill in our family life a deep sense of meaning for Jesus's birth that put Christmas morning in perspective. In the midst of the presents, special cookies, and homemade sticky buns we knew that the true meaning of Christmas wasn't wrapped up in a box under the tree. Rather, it was wrapped up in the miraculous event of Jesus' birth, represented by the advent of Jesus appearing in the manger of our Creche on the fireplace mantel.

I hope I have encouraged you to take the four or five weeks before Christmas to dive deeper into its meaning. To that end, here are four devotionals that you might consider doing with your family. We typically read our Advent devotions after dinner, but there is not one special time that is better than another. Simply taking the time as a family to redirect your attention to Jesus and His Advent will leave an impression with your children that they will take into their adulthood. Ours did, and what a joy to continue celebrating with them.

Week One

December is a great time of year: children are getting excited about Christmas; parents are frantically looking for the best shopping deals for gifts; college students cannot wait for their final exams to be complete; families are scouring for the best-looking Christmas tree. And in the midst of the hustle and bustle of the season, we are reminded that Jesus was born.

And in the same region there were shepherds out in the field, keeping watch over their flock by night. And an angel of the Lord appeared to them, and the glory of the Lord shone around them, and they were filled with great fear. And the angel said to them, "Fear not, for behold, I bring you good news of great joy that will be for all the people. For unto you is born this day in the city of David a Savior, who is Christ the Lord. And this will be a sign for you: you will find a baby wrapped in swaddling cloths and lying in a manger." And suddenly there was with the angel a multitude of the heavenly host praising God and saying, "Glory to God in the highest, and on earth peace among those with whom he is pleased!" (Luke 2:8-14)

That first Christmas must have been incredible. It was an announcement like no other to a group of people who were of no consequence. Whatever great fear feels like, it must have been intense for those shepherds. Here they were with their sheep at night in pitch-black darkness that would have been illumined only by the stars. The shepherds, ever so vigilant and constantly on alert from all sides, would have, at times, encountered fierce wolves surrounding their prey in the cover of darkness. With courage and bravery, they successfully thwarted many attacks by these predators.

On this night, however, they were filled with terror like nothing they had ever experienced. Heaven had opened up. They were all at once surrounded! But, not by wolves. It was the glory of God Himself, shining down on them with the announcement of good news for all people. It was the ultimate Christmas card, delivered in the most awesome manner and it would change their great fear into great joy.

After more than 2,000 years, that Good News is still being delivered here and around the world. Sometimes we hear stories of the gospel coming to Muslims and Hindus through the announcement of a messenger in a dream or vision. More often, the gospel is shared through personal testimonies of faithful Christians, like you and me, who have experienced the great joy of the Savior. And it always brings God glory when the announcement is shared with others.

In the midst of the hustle and bustle of the season, the story of the shepherds reminds us to be aware that there are people we will encounter at work, in our neighborhoods, on the airplane, or at the shopping mall who might be overwhelmed with great fear but ready to hear the Good News of great joy that is for them.

Week Two

Joseph and his betrothed, Mary, arrived in Bethlehem some time before Jesus's birth. They traveled the eight-day journey along the Jordan River from Nazareth most likely with a caravan as there were always dangers along those roads. Luke tells us that once they arrived in the city of their ancestors, they could not find a room. So, other accommodations were made to provide for an obviously pregnant relative. Then, He was born.

We tend to add more to the Christmas story, such as Mary traveling on a donkey, although it is hard to imagine a pregnant woman on the back of a beast of burden for eight days. Or, the birth occurring in a stable, even though stables were not in use in Palestine at the time. We add the inn keeper who said there were no vacancies, although inns would not have been in a city such as Bethlehem. We even add a cold December night to the birth, though shepherds would hardly be keeping watch of sheep outside in winter. These things add color to the story of Jesus's birth, although they are not mentioned in Scripture.

Erwin Lutzer, former pastor of Moody Bible Church in Chicago, once said something to the effect that there would be no cross if there were not a cradle. While true, there is a certain cuteness to the image of a cradle surrounded by animals with Mary and Joseph kneeling on a bed of straw in a stable gazing at their newborn Son under the glow of a star as shepherds and three wise men arrive with gifts. However, the actual story is much more profound.

> *When the angels went away from them into heaven, the shepherds said to one another, "Let us go over to Bethlehem and see this thing that has happened, which the Lord has made known to us." And they went with haste and found Mary and Joseph, and the baby lying in a manger. And when they saw it, they made known the saying that had been told them concerning this child. And all who heard it wondered at what the shepherds told them. But Mary treasured up all these things, pondering them in her heart. And the shepherds returned, glorifying and praising God for all they had heard and seen, as it had been told them. (Luke 2:15-20)*

The shepherds' great fear had been turned to great joy and their great joy would turn to great praise. So, they go "with haste" to find what they had heard from the angel. Christ the Lord, the Son of God, was indeed born! And there He was, exactly like the angel had announced. The color we sometimes add to the story of the birth of our Savior can distract us from what Scripture says: the shepherds found Jesus just as they had been told. What the angel announced was indeed true! Christ had come! A Savior was born! God took on human form!

We have no idea how many babies had been born in Bethlehem at this time or on this day, but His was different. He alone was lying in a manger wrapped in swaddling cloth. And if this were true, as the shepherds experienced, then He must be the Savior.

Just as in the field after the angelic announcement when the chorus sang, "Glory to God in the highest," so now the shepherds, departing from the child, sang in praise. It was all about God's glory! The great Giver gave a great Gift that brought great joy and resulted in great praise.

So, here's a question that has challenged us during this season. What would happen if we genuinely understood that Christmas was about God's glory? How would that change our lives? It changed the shepherds. From their great joy swelled great praise to God and they told everyone about their incredible experience.

Week Three

It is hard to imagine their situation. Nine months before, Mary was young, unmarried, and told she would become pregnant, an even greater miracle than what had happened with her relative Elizabeth. She learned from Gabriel that her baby would be Great and would be called the Son of the Most High. He would rule from the throne of David over the house of Jacob, and His kingdom would have no end. Joseph was honorable yet understandably perplexed when reassured by an angel in a dream that Mary's pregnancy was by the Holy Spirit. They were both told the same thing: to name the baby Jesus.

And at the end of eight days, when He was circumcised, He was called Jesus, the name given by the angel before He was conceived in the womb. (Luke 2:21)

The Apostle Peter tells us that there is no other name under heaven by which we can be saved (Acts

4:12). It is the Name that is above every name and at the sound of that Name, the Apostle Paul tells us, every knee will bow and tongue confess that He is Lord (Phil 2:9-10). His Hebrew name means "God saves" and it is that Name, the one given to Him by Mary and Joseph, we proclaim around the world. An Arab Christian recently shared,

> *I understand that Jesus is the only way to go to heaven and receive a blessing from God. I confessed my sins before God and I cry to Him for my sins. I have peace in my heart and understand that Jesus forgave my sins. I accepted Jesus as my personal Savior and Lord and decided to follow Him. I started to read my Bible regularly and pray to God. Now, I am sharing about God with other Muslims among our own people and through me many people accepted Jesus as their Savior and Lord and are obeying the word of God. I want to give thanks to God that He has chosen me for His kingdom. I give all glory and honor to Jesus because He is my Lord whom I worship day and night. Jesus is my Heart. I love Jesus because He loved me first.*

A wonderful testimony of how God saves, yet, it is hard to imagine that there are still places on the planet that have never heard the name of Jesus. More than two millennia after the angelic announcement of Good News of great joy that is for a great many, not all have heard. In 1900, there were only 880 million people who did not know the name of Jesus. Today, because of population growth, there are 2.1 billion who have never heard the name that Mary and Joseph gave their newborn baby. Even so, the proclamation of that name brings great joy for a great many. Now, it is for us to proclaim it to a great many more.

Week Four

And here they were: about forty days after Jesus's birth, Mary and Joseph went to Jerusalem to present Him to God as their first born. It was a part of the Jewish law passed down since the time of Moses.

Now there was a man in Jerusalem, whose name was Simeon, and this man was righteous and devout, waiting for the consolation of Israel, and the Holy Spirit was upon him. And it had been revealed to him by the Holy Spirit that he would not see death before he had seen the Lord's Christ. And he came in the Spirit into the temple, and when the parents brought in the child Jesus, to do for him according to the custom of the Law, he took him up in his arms and blessed God and said, "Lord, now you are letting your servant depart in peace, according to your word; for my eyes have seen your salvation that you have prepared in the presence of all peoples, a light for revelation to the [nations], and for glory to your people Israel." And his father and his mother marveled at what was said about him. (Luke 2:25-33)

The angel announced Him. The shepherds praised Him. Mary and Joseph named Him. And now, Simeon proclaims God's salvation. The God who saves, Jesus, is the Good News of great joy. Just as the angel announced and Simeon proclaims, that Good News is for all people. Even though we live in a world today where there are still nearly 1,000 ethnic groups who have never had contact with someone who could tell them the Good News of great joy, we know one day they will hear. The Apostle John tells us,

And they sang a new song, saying, "Worthy are you [Jesus] to take the scroll   and to open its seals, for you were slain, and by your blood you ransomed people for God from every tribe and language and people and nation, and you have made them a kingdom and priests to our God, and they shall reign on the earth." (Rev 5:9-10)

The blessing of Christmas is not about what happened this morning around the Christmas tree, even though the giving of gifts, the love we feel for our family and friends, the hope for peace, and the traditions we celebrate emanate from those magnificent events surrounding the birth of Jesus more than 2,000 years ago. The great blessing of the Christmas story is God invading human history as a precious baby to give Himself so that others could also see His salvation, just like Simeon. Now, just like Simeon, we have the privilege to proclaim Him to every tribe, language, people, and nation.

We pray that this Christmas will indeed be a great blessing in knowing the great joy that is for us all.

A Baby Changes Everything

We come to the end of this little book and hopefully a richer understanding of the first Christmas. As I mentioned, the birth of Christ is the single most amazing event in human history. I know many might argue that Jesus's death and resurrection fit that bill much more appropriately. However, Greek philosophers prior to Jesus's arrival were expecting some sort of resurrection of the dead. The Jewish Pharisees were as well, something that distinguished them from the Sadducees, their intellectual and religious counterparts.

No one could have anticipated who the Apostle John eventually called the Word made flesh, who is God Himself (John 1:14). Others might argue that there were god-man figures such as in the mystery religions of the Middle East and North Africa who were the progeny of human women and male gods. The dating of any reliable sources to authenticate such belief does not appear until well into the Christian era, examples of Pagan religions borrowing from Christianity.

As for Jesus Himself, very few scholars believe that He was born on 25 December but even fewer would actually discount the event altogether. There is simply too much external attestation to His historicity. As I once wrote,

> *The significance of the issue addressing New Testament reliability cannot be underestimated. For one, the pre 70AD dating of the New Testament synoptic gospels and Acts clearly establishes an early belief in the [birth and] resurrection of Christ and the performance of signs and wonders. These early beliefs were circulated and could be confirmed by eyewitnesses. Not only does the reliability of the New Testament testify to early beliefs, it also testifies to the claims that Christ made about himself. Therefore, it is significant that when Christ claimed to be God, we have a reliable witness to his claim and eyewitnesses could confirm it. While the [Pagan] mystery religions hoped for new birth, signs and wonders and the resurrection of the dead, it is only in Christianity that we see fulfillment. (Cooper 2005:185-186)*

Jesus's uniqueness is still what draws many people to explore His remarkable life. This unique life is the central point of the Christmas story:

- Jesus is unique because many wrote about Him hundreds of years before His birth. Not only do we learn about Jesus in from Jewish prophets, but also from Greek philosophers like Heraclitus.

- His birth is unique as He was born by a virgin. Between 7-4BC, there was no other religious myth that made such a claim.

- His life is unique in that He lived without sin, proving that He is God.

- His work is unique as He performed miracles which had never been seen before.

- His death is unique because He did nothing to deserve it.

- His resurrection is unique because it demonstrated God's power over death and His ability to grant eternal life to those who believe.

Jesus provides an inclusive manner by which anyone can enter into a relationship with God indifferent of culture and ethnicity. The proof of His ability to bring humanity to God is His incarnation and resurrection. So, just as the shepherds and Magi came to worship the newborn King, Jesus desires for us all to experience the Good News that is for all people,

> *For God so loved the world that He gave His only Son, that whoever believes in Him should not perish but have eternal life. For God did not send His Son into the world to condemn the world, but in order that the world might be saved through Him. Whoever believes in Him is not condemned, but whoever does not believe is condemned already, because he has not believed in the name of the only Son of God. (John 3:16-18)*

I hope your future Christmases will be fuller as you continue to unwrap the first Christmas. Perhaps this book has helped a bit. At least, that is my prayer.

Appendix

In case you are curious, here is my rationale for the answers to the Christmas test.

1) What did the angel Gabriel say to Joseph?

Answer: Nothing – Matthew doesn't tell us which angel it was who spoke to Joseph, just that an angel of the Lord appeared to him (Matt 1:20).

2) What mode of transportation did Mary and Joseph take to Bethlehem?

Answer: Don't know – the Bible doesn't mention any mode of transportation for the couple (Luke 2:4).

3) Who told Joseph that there was no room at the Inn?

Answer: No one – Mary and Joseph arrived in Bethlehem and learned that there was not an available room. The Christmas story does not say who told them (Luke 2:7).

4)   Where in Bethlehem was Jesus born?

Answer: In a manger, but we don't know where – this one is a bit more challenging due to the English translation which typically says that there was no place at the inn. However, the Greek word in Luke 2:7 translated "inn" is *katalyma* or literally a guest room. It is the same word used in Luke 22:11 and Mark 14:14, the place where Jesus met His disciples for the Passover meal. Since Mary and Joseph are both from the line of David and their relatives lived in Bethlehem, it seems reasonable to suggest that a relative took them into their home. With all the relatives in Bethlehem at the same time, it makes perfect sense that there was no place in the guest room.

5)   When did Mary give birth to Jesus?

Answer: After a few days upon their arrival in Bethlehem – Luke 2:6 simply tells us that Mary gave birth at some point while they were in Bethlehem.

6)   How many wise men brought gifts and visited Jesus?

Answer: Don't know (Matt 2:1) – we often assume three wise men because of the three gifts of gold, frankincense, and myrrh (Matt 2:11).

7)   Where did the wise men visit Jesus?

Answer: In a house in Bethlehem – Matt 2:11 tells us that the wise men went to a house and found Mary with Jesus. This makes perfect sense and dove tails with questions 3 and 4. After all, would you allow your pregnant relative to give birth in a dirty stable?

8)   How long did Joseph and Mary stay in Bethlehem?

Answer: 40 days – Luke 2:22 tells us that the time of purification had come, and Jesus was presented at the temple in Jerusalem, which ties to the next question.

9)   Where did Mary and Joseph go after Jesus' birth?

Answer: To Jerusalem – we often think that the flight of the family to Egypt happened immediately after Jesus' birth, but Scripture indicates that Mary and

Joseph presented Jesus in the temple 40 days after his birth according to Jewish law (Lev 12:2—8).

10) Why did Jesus come to earth?

Answer: All of the above – The heavenly host declared peace on earth (Luke 2:14); the angel tells Joseph that Jesus would save His people from their sins (Matt 2:21); and Luke 19:10 tells us that He seeks and saves that which is lost.

Reference List

Augustine. 1989. *Harmony of the Gospels*. In *Nicene and Post—Nicene Fathers*, Vol. VI, ed. Phillip Schaff, 73—240. Peabody, Mass.: Hendrickson.

Basil. 2004. *On the Spirit*. In *Nicene and Post—Nicene Fathers*, vol. VIII, ed. Philip Schaff and Henry Wace, 2—50. Grand Rapids: Hendrickson.

Bede, The Venerable. 1983. *The Ecclesiastical History of the English Nation*, ed. Cecil Jane. Mobile, Ala.: RE Publications.

Boniface. *The Letters of Saint Boniface*, trans. Emerton, Ephraim. New York: W.W. Norton & Company.

Brown, Peter. 1967. *Augustine of Hippo: A Biography*. Berkeley, Calif.: University of California Press.

Chapman, Colin. 1990. *Shadows of the Supernatural: A Guide to Popular Religion*. Oxford: Lion.

Clark, Charles. 2001. "A Christian Defense of Astrology in the Twelfth Century: The Liber Cursuum

Planetarum of Raymond of Marseilles." *International Social Science Review* 70, no. 3–4: 93–94.

Cooper, Michael T. 2020. *Ephesiology: The Study of a Movement*. Littleton, CO: William Carey Publishers.

__________. 2007. "New Testament Astral Portents: God's Self—Disclosure in the Heavens." *Journal of Religion, Nature, and Culture* 1, no. 2: 189–209.

__________. 2005. "Jesus and the Pagan West: Missiological Reflections on Evangelism in Re—enchanted Europe." In *The Centrality of Christ in Contemporary Missions*. Mike Barnett and Michael Pocock, eds. Littleton, CO: William Carey Publishers, 165–194.

Eddy, Paul Rhodes and Gregory A. Boyd. 2007. *The Jesus Legend: A Case for the Historical Reliability of the Synoptic Jesus Tradition*. Grand Rapids: Baker Academic.

Ellis, Peter Berresford. 1994. *A Brief History of the Druids*. Grand Rapids: Eerdmans.

English, Adam C. 2018. *The Saint Who Would be Santa Claus: The True Life and Trails of Nicholas of Myra*. Waco: Baylor University.

Filotas, Bernadette. 2005. *Pagan Survivals, Superstitions and Popular Cultures in Early Medieval Pastoral Literature*. Toronto: Pontifical Institute of Mediaeval Studies.

Frazer, Sir James George. 1922. *The Golden Bough: A Study of Magic and Religion*, [book online] New York: Macmillan. Accessed 21 July 2003. Available from www.bartleby.com/196/. Internet.

Frend, W. H. C. 1984. *The Rise of Christianity*. Philadelphia: Fortress.

Hillgarth, J. N. 1987. "Modes of Evangelization of Western Europe in the Seventh Century." In *Irland und die Christenheit: Bibelstudien und Mission*, ed. Proinseas Ni Chathain and Michael Richter, 325—327. Stuttgart: Klett—Cotta.

Hutton, Ronald 1991. *The Pagan Religions of the Ancient British Isles: Their Nature and Legacy*. London: Blackwell.

__________. 1996. *The Stations of the Sun: A History of the Ritual Year in Britain*. Oxford: Oxford University.

__________. 2003. "Astral Magic: The Acceptable Face of Paganism," Lecture given at the inaugural conference of the Sophia Centre, Bath Spa University College "Astrology and the Academy," 13 June.

Ignatius of Antioch. 1999. *Letter to the Ephesians.* In *Ante-Nicene Fathers: The Writings of the Fathers Down to AD 325*, Vol. 1, ed. Alexander Roberts and James Donaldson, 49–58. Peabody, Mass.: Hendrickson.

Jones, Prudence. 1998. "The European Native Tradition." In *Nature Religion Today: Paganism in the Modern World*, ed. Joanne Pearson, Richard H. Roberts and Geoffrey Samuel, 77–88. Edinburgh: Edinburgh University.

Jones, Prudence and Nigel Pennick. 1995. *A History of Pagan Europe*. London: Routledge.

Josephus, Flavius. Antiquities.

Kidger, Mark. 1999. *The Star of Bethlehem: An Astronomer's View*. Princeton: Princeton University Press.

Marshall, I. Howard. 1978. *The Gospel of Luke*. Exeter: Paternoster.

Michael the Archimandrite. N.d. *Life, Works, and Miracles of Our Holy Father Nicholas, Archbishop of Myra in Lycia.* Available from:

https://www.stnicholascenter.org/who-is-st-nicholas/stories-legends/classic-sources/michael-the-archimandrite

Molnar, Michael. 1999. *The Star of Bethlehem: The Legacy of the Magi*. Rutgers University Press.

Morris, Leon. 1997. *Luke: An Introduction and Commentary*. Grand Rapids: Eerdmans.

Pliny, *Natural History*.

Ptolemy, Claudius. 1940. *Tetrabiblos*. Trans. by F.E. Robbins. Cambridge, Mass.: Harvard.

Toepel, Alexander. 2005. "Planetary Demons in Early Jewish Literature," *Journal for the Study of the Pseudepigrapha*, 14, 3: 231.

Trexler, Richard. 1997. *The Journey of the Magi: Meanings in History of a Christian Story*. Princeton: Princeton University Press.

Vettius Valens. *Anthology*.

Von Stuckrad, Kocku. 2000. "Jewish and Christian Astrology in Late Antiquity – a New Approach," *Numen*, vol. 47:2–3.

Wallace—Hadrill, J. M. 1988. *Bede's Ecclesiastical History of the English People: A Historical Commentary*. Oxford: Clarendon.

Zacharias. *Epistles*.

About the Author

Dr. Cooper earned a PhD in Intercultural Studies with a focus on religious movements and a minor in theology from Trinity Evangelical Divinity School. He currently serves as a missiologist for East West Ministries International where he focuses on missiological research and equipping missionaries for effective cultural engagement. He has thirty years of missions experience, including ten years as a pioneer church planter in Romania after the fall of communism and has equipped church planters and leaders in Africa, Europe, North America, South America, South Asia, and Southeast Asia. He has written and contributed to more than 30 books and academic articles and has presented conference lectures at the London School of Economics, University of Bordeaux, Loyola University, Baylor University, Arab Baptist Theological Seminary, Torch Trinity Graduate University, and many others. His recent book, *Ephesiology: The Study of the Ephesian Movement* is a best seller at William Carey Publishing.

To learn more about Michael's work and the work of Ephesiology Master Classes, you can contact them at info@ephesiology.com.

Other Books by Michael

When Evangelicals Sneeze: Curing the American Church of the Plague of Identity Loss. Ephesiology Press, 2020.

Ephesiology: The Study of a Movement. Littleton: William Carey Publishing, 2020.

God's Mission in the World: A Simple Study of the Bible's Grand Narrative for Oral Learners. Ephesiology Press, 2019.

Editor (with William J. Moulder) and Contributor, *Social Injustice: What Evangelicals Need to Know about the World.* Lake Forest: The Timothy Center Press, 2011.

Editor (with Clifford Williams) and Contributor, *The Peaceable Christian: Five Evangelicals Reflect on Peace*. Lake Forest: The Timothy Center Press, 2011.

Contemporary Druidry: A Historical and Ethnographic Study. Salt Lake City: Sacred Tribes Press, 2010.

Editor and Contributor, *Perspectives on Post—Christendom Spiritualties: Reflections on New Religious Movements and Western Spiritualities*. Sydney, Australia: Morling Press, 2010.

About Ephesiology

Ephesiology focuses on the study of the early Christian movement that began in the city of Ephesus. Ephesus was the site of the most significant church-planting movement in the early church, with 40 percent of the New Testament texts relating to it. What made that city the epicenter of the movement? And how can we replicate sustained movements in a world that feels so different? Learn more at https://ephesiology.com

Ephesiology Podcast

Join our podcasters each week for a captivating discussion about a New Testament movement that started in Ephesus and impacted all of Asia Minor for 13 centuries. We dig deeply into the missiological theology of the New Testament in order to understand what a movement might look like today. Find us on your favorite podcast app.

Looking for a Speaker?

All of our topics can be either in person or via video webinar. Contact us for more information.

Business Luncheon – typically a 30-45 minute talk focused on engaging the business community in the completion of the Great Commission. For audiences of all sizes.

Church Leaders' Luncheon – typically a 30-45 minute talk focused on casting vision for a missiologically theocentric passion for God's glory by joining His mission in pursuit of more worshipers. For audiences of all sizes.

Sermon – typically a 30-45 minute exegetical sermon focused on one of the following topics: launching a movement, grounding a movement, leading a movement, multiplying a movement, or sustaining a movement.

Shepherding Your Church to Movement – one day seminar focused on a missiologically theocentric ecclesiology expressed in four salient features: praxis, koinonia, hermeneutics, leaders. We also design a unique online interactive experience for participants. For audiences of all sizes.

Movement Workshop – a two-day workshop focused on discovering principles of a missiologically theocentric movement that effectively engages a community by connecting Jesus's story to the story of the people. The workshop culminates in a movement action plan uniquely designed to engage your community, disciple new believers, develop leaders, and establish healthy communities of Christ-followers. Includes a free copy of *Ephesiology: The Study of the Ephesian Movement*. Limited to 20 key leaders.

Learn more at https://ephesiology.com/welcome-to-ephesiology/host-an-ephesiologist/

Ephesiology Master Classes

An Ephesiology Master Class is not your typical seminary course. In fact, this is learning designed with you in mind. Our classes are especially designed for an online and engaging experience that is focused on your learning goals.

Since we have been where you are, we focus on content that we know will help you succeed in multiplying disciples, planting churches, and crossing cultures.

Focused on those who want the missions and ministry skills without the price tag of a seminary, we have designed a platform that is accessible 24/7 from anywhere in the world and will not put you in debt. The collaborative nature of our classes will enhance the sense of community where innovation and creativity can thrive. This is a learning experience designed with the practitioner in mind.

Ephesiology Master Classes

Here's Where You Cultivate a Passion for God's Mission

If you are going to shape today's dreamers into tomorrow's leaders who multiply Christ-followers and lead God-glorifying movements then your journey starts here. Let us show you the way.

Use coupon code CHRISTMAS2020 for a 10% discount on *Unwrapping for First Christmas* enrichment master class.

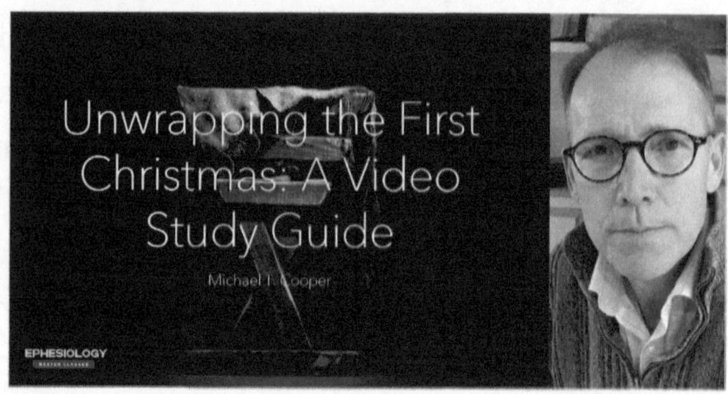